WITHDRAWN
L. R. COLLEGE LIBRARY

WITHDRAWN
L. R. COLLEGE LIBRARY

W9-BJV-304

DRAMATIZED RHYTHM PLAYS

MOTHER GOOSE AND TRADITIONAL

BY

JOHN N. RICHARDS, B. P. E.

ASSISTANT SUPERVISOR OF PHYSICAL EDUCATION
NEWARK, N. J.

NEW YORK

A. S. BARNES AND COMPANY

1931

Lenoir Rhyne Colleg
LIBRARY

796.1
R39d

16,391

Copyright, 1922,

BY

A. S. BARNES AND COMPANY

This book is fully protected by copyright and nothing
that appears in it may be reprinted or reproduced in
any manner, either wholly or in part, for any use
whatever, without special written permission of the
copyright owner.

PRINTED IN THE UNITED STATES OF AMERICA

796.1
R39d

NO TRIM
Bottom

PREFACE

The following rhythmic plays compiled by Mr. John N. Richards of the Newark Department of Physical Education have been devised to meet the needs in the transition of Physical Education activities between the kindergarten and the first few years of the primary school.

The physiologist tells us that the nervous organism of early childhood is injured by the strain of strict, immobile attention required in formal gymnastics. Therefore it is wise to hold the child's interest and attention by means of dramatized nursery plays. These make little strain on mental application and the child is able to dramatize in motion the words and music which are planned to develop his motor co-ordination. In this way the child is gradually and interestingly led from the freedom of expression, characteristic of babyhood to the more specialized formal activities of the third and fourth years in the school.

Mr. Richards' contribution merits widespread usage because he has clearly and definitely described his rhythm plays so that the classroom teacher can easily make use of them without having to draw on her imagination or having to guess at the written explanation.

The book should be useful and welcomed too, not only by the classroom teacher but also by the specialist and supervisor of Physical Education.

Randall D. Warden

Director of Physical Education, Newark, N. J., Public Schools

INTRODUCTION

The young people of to-day are most fortunate in their opportunities and advantages. The home, the school, the shop, social life and play offer increasing fields for service. The ever increasing number of problems which must be faced, in this reconstruction period of our nation's life, demands leaders of broad intellect, clear vision and sound judgment. Coupled with these qualifications there must be developed a moral earnestness which will make for better citizenship.

The trend of society movement is undoubtedly toward congested city life. There is lamentable lack of playgrounds and properly equipped gymnasiums. The school buildings are crowded to capacity and there is a rush and hurry of life which challenges the attention of all educators who are interested in the physical well-being of children.

The priceless assets of our communities are the boys and girls who are growing into manhood and womanhood. We should spare neither expense nor energy in fitting them physically, mentally and spiritually for the great problems which will all too soon be theirs.

Exercise habits and a spirit of fair play must be a part of their training from the early school days. There is no better way of inculcating these lessons than through story plays and games during their first school years.

The material contained in this book is practical. The exercise movements have been set to music which is popular both in the schools and in the homes. It is carefully graded and should prove to be of great assistance to the teachers in the lower grades. It tends to bridge over the gap between the Kindergarten and the Primary Grade activities.

There is need for a manual of this type in our Physical Training literature and it is hoped that this material will be used generally throughout the schools of our country.

F. W. Maroney, M.D.

Director of Physical Education and Medical Inspection
Atlantic City, N. J., Public Schools

ACKNOWLEDGMENTS

———

The author wishes to express his thanks to F. W. Maroney, M.D., formerly Director of Physical Education of the State of New Jersey and now Director of Physical Education and Medical Inspection of the Public Schools of Atlantic City, N. J., for the Introduction.

To Mr. Randall D. Warden, Director of Physical Education, Public Schools, Newark, N. J., for the Preface.

Special acknowledgment and thanks are due Miss A. E. Barth of the Charlton Street School, Newark, N. J., for her contribution of "Rhythm Plays" and to Miss Louise Westwood, Director of Music, Newark Public Schools, as hereinafter stated.

Thanks are also due to McLoughlin Bros. for permission to use the words and music of the following songs found in J. W. Elliott's book entitled, "Nursery Rhymes, Set to Music":

Little Jack Horner   Dickory, Dickory, Dock
See Saw, Marjory Daw   Sing a Song of Sixpence
Humpty Dumpty

To D. Appleton & Company for permission to use the words and music of the following songs found in "Songs the Whole World Sings":

Rock-a-bye, Baby   Little Boy Blue

To Miss Lydia Clark, author of "Physical Training for Elementary Schools," and to B. H. Sanborn & Company, for permission to use the words and music of the following songs:

Where Has My Little Dog Gone?   Baa, Baa, Black Sheep
Looby Loo

J. N. Richards

ALPHABETICAL INDEX

Aisles of Classroom

Circle

GRADATION INDEX

INDEX OF PROGRESSION

Aisles of Classroom

Circle

(Outer aisles of classroom)

SUGGESTIONS FOR THE TEACHING OF THE GYMNASTIC ACTIVITY

1. Teach the words of the rhyme to the class, keeping in mind the rhythm.

2. If in presenting the action, the movement is based upon certain words as cues, present by imitation the activity as applied to the words, *i. e.*, Little Jack Horner; Little Miss Muffet, etc.

3. If the movement is based on a time element (rhythm), present the activity content, line by line, *i.e.*, Yankee Doodle; Pat-a-cake, etc.

4. Be sure the rhyme and activity has been thoroughly mastered before adding the song element.

5. If a dancing movement is involved, present same to the class as a unit before combining with other movements, *i.e.*, Fly Away Jack and Jill; Diddle, Diddle, Dumpling, etc.

The author wishes to express thanks to Miss Louise Westwood, Director of Music of the Newark Public Schools, for the following suggestions as to the teaching of the song element:

1. Pitch-pipes:

No song under any condition should be sung without the pitch of the first word being given; using the pitch-pipe to get the key in which the song is written.

2. Range of Songs:

All songs should be sung not lower than the first line E or higher than the fifth line F of the staff. If songs are scored in another range, transpose the song by changing the pitch of the *first* word.

3. Quality of Tone:

All singing should be in a soft, light, head tone. Half-tone quality.
No loud singing should be allowed at any time.

PROCEDURE IN TEACHING

1. Teach the rhyme. 2. Combine rhyme with the gymnastic activity.
3. Teach the song. 4. Combine No. 1, No. 2 and No. 3.

COMMANDS USED TO PRESENT THE GYMNASTIC ACTIVITY AND SONG

1. Determine key in which the song is written and find starting note.
2. Teacher sounds keynote of first syllable or word.
Command:—Pitch—Sing!

Examples:

(a) Yankee Doodle. The first syllable of the word, "Yankee," which is "Yank," is sung to establish the pitch.

(b) Oh, where, oh where has my little dog gone? The first word, "Oh," is sung to establish the pitch.

3. In order to insure united action, the following command is used:
Ready—Begin!

RHYTHMIC STEPS

1. The Point Step, Forward:

Point foot forward with outside edge of toes touching the floor; the heel is raised and turned inward toward the other foot. (No weight transference, the weight being on the stationary foot.)

2. Closing Step, Sideward:

Step sideward, right, maintaining the weight equally to both feet (1). Close left foot to right (2).

Note.—Counterlike for movement in the forward and backward direction.

3. Chasse or Gliding Step, Sideward:

Raise heels and slide sideward, right, immediately closing left to right. A light, quick movement requiring only one count for completion.

4. Step Throw or Step Hop Swing, Sideward:

Step sideward, right (1). Hop on right, and swing left leg diagonally forward across (2). (Knee slightly flexed with ankle extended.)

5. Schottische Step, Sideward:

Step sideward, right (1). Cross step left to rear of right (2). Step sideward, right (3). Hop on right, swinging left leg diagonally forward across (4). (Knee slightly flexed with ankle extended.)

6. Two Step or Change Step, Forward:

Step forward, right (1). Close left instep to right heel (and) Step forward, right (2).

7. The Step Dip, Sideward:

Step sideward, right, with transference of body weight to the right foot (1). Place left toe behind right heel (heel raised) with the knee turned sideward (and) Bend and stretch right knee slightly with trunk bending sideward, left (2).

Hand clapping occurs on counts *one and two.*

8. Encircle to left with partner kneeling. (Partners.)

Stationary pupil.—Pupil extends leg backward, lowering knee to floor. The trunk is erect; left hand on hip with the right arm stretched upward, supporting encircling partner's left hand.

Dancing pupil.—The encircling pupil grasps with the left hand the kneeling partner's right hand and performs the dance movement in given direction.

DIAGRAMMATIC FORMATIONS

Classroom

Standing in the right aisle facing front of room.

Six rows of seats; six pupils per row.

Classroom

Standing in the right aisle in OPEN LINE FORMATION, partners facing.

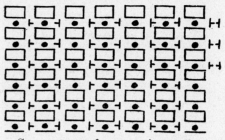

Seven rows of seats; six pupils per row.

NOTE:—When executing partner plays, children in extreme row on the right (odd row) form in partner formation in open area.

Circular

SINGLE

Facing, line of direction.

Counter-clockwise

Facing, inward.

Facing, reverse line of direction.

Clockwise

DOUBLE

Facing, line of direction.

Facing, reverse line of direction.

Partner formation, facing each other.

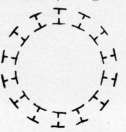

CLASSROOM

Aisle Alignment:—Single and partner formation.

Note:—May also be used to advantage in any open area or gymnasium with exception of several in the First Grade which are essentially classroom in type. (Desks are used as part of the rhythmic action.)

THE BAND

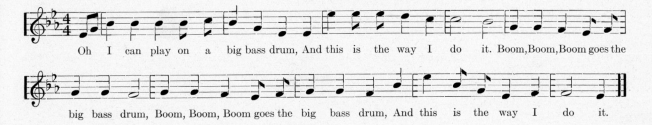

Oh I can play on a big bass drum, And this is the way I do it. Boom, Boom, Boom goes the

big bass drum, Boom, Boom, Boom goes the big bass drum, And this is the way I do it.

DESCRIPTION

Miss A. E. Barth.

Formation;—Children seated in their seats.

1st Line;—Oh I can play on a big bass drum,
Interpretation;—No activity.

2nd Line;—And this is the way I do it.
Inter.;—   No activity.

3rd Line;—Boom, Boom, Boom goes the big bass drum,
Inter.;—   Beat hands vigorously upon top of desks, suiting action to the words.

4th Line;—Boom, Boom, Boom goes the big bass drum.
Inter.;—   Repeat the activity of the third line.

5th Line;—And this is the way I do it.
Inter.;—   Repeat the activity of the fourth line.

Introduce the following activities, suiting the action to the words in imitation of the suggested activity.

Little Snare Drum ("Trum")   Big Brass Horn ("Toot")
Little Gay Flute ("Whistle")

OH I CAN PLAY ON A BIG BRASS HORN

LITTLE JACK HORNER

Permission to use words and music:—McLoughlin Bros.

J. W. ELLIOTT

Lit-tle Jack Hor-ner sat in a cor-ner, Eat-ing a Christ-mas pie; He put in his thumb, and

pulled out a plum, And said, "What a good boy am I!" Nice Plum! Nice Plum! Nice Plum! Nice Plum!

DESCRIPTION

MISS A. E. BARTH

Formation;—Children remain seated and move to the right side of seat.

1st Line;—Little Jack Horner sat in a corner,

Interpretation;—Upon the word, "sat," pupils move to the left side of seat.

2nd Line;—Eating a Christmas pie;

Inter.;— Upon the word, "eating," pupils encircle imaginary plate with the left arm and imitate eating with the right hand.

3rd Line;—He put in his thumb, And pulled out a plum,

Inter.;— Upon the word, "put," pupil imitates the action of putting thumb in pie and pulling out a plum, making the action vigorous upon the word, "pulled," stretching the arm overhead. Looks at the plum.

4th Line;—And said, "What a good boy am I!"

Inter.;— Proudly pats the chest with the left hand.

Conclusion;—Nice Plum! Nice Plum! Nice Plum! Nice Plum!

Inter.;— Lowers plum until it disappears in the mouth, imitating eating, tapping his chest the while.

HE PUT IN HIS THUMB, AND PULLED OUT A PLUM

ROCK - A - BYE, BABY

Permission to use words and music:—D. Appleton and Co.

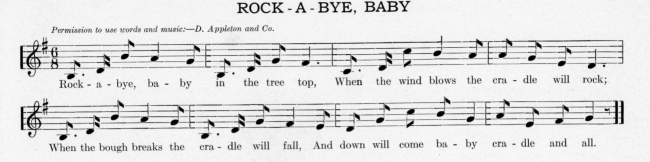

Rock - a - bye, ba - by in the tree top, When the wind blows the cra - dle will rock;

When the bough breaks the cra - dle will fall, And down will come ba - by cra - dle and all.

DESCRIPTION

Miss A. E. Barth

Formation;—Standing in the right aisle at attention.

1st Line;—Rock-a-bye, baby in the tree top,

Interpretation;—Hold baby in the arms, looking down at it, and sway gently to and fro. (Right; left; right and left.)

2nd Line;—When the wind blows the cradle will rock;

Inter.;— Rock more vigorously.

3rd Line;—When the bough breaks the cradle will fall,

Inter.;— Upon the word, "breaks," children clap hands overhead—partially dropping the baby.

4th Line;—And down will come baby, cradle and all.

Inter.;— Upon the word, "down," children spring into the air and immediately assume deep knee bending position.

Position.

ROCKING THE BABY

JACK BE NIMBLE—No. 1

Arr. by J. N. Richards

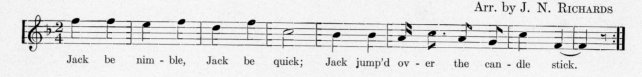

Jack be nim - ble, Jack be quick; Jack jump'd ov - er the can - dle stick.

DESCRIPTION

Miss A. E. Barth

Formation;—Standing in the right aisle with hands on hips.

1st Line;—Jack be nimble, Jack be quick;

Interpretation;—Marking time, in place. (Seven counts.)

2nd Line;—Jack jumped over the candle stick.

Inter.;— Upon the word, "jumped," the children face to the left and vault over their own seats; finish facing the front of room with hands on hips.

Repeat rhyme and activity back to former aisle.

JACK JUMPED OVER THE CANDLE STICK

JACK BE NIMBLE—No. 2

Music—*See Jack Be Nimble—No. 1*

DESCRIPTION

Formation;—Standing in the right aisle with hands on hips.

1st Line;—Jack be

Interpretation;—With a jump execute ¼ turn to the left.

nimble

With a jump execute ¼ turn to the right. (Front.)

2nd Line;—Jack be

Inter.;— With a jump execute ¼ turn to the right.

quick;

With a jump execute ¼ turn to the left. (Front.)

3rd Line;—Jack

Inter.;— One-quarter turn to the left, placing hands on the near edge of desk and back of seat, bending knees slightly.

jumped over

Vault over the seat; replace hands to hips and execute ¼ turn to the right (Front.)

4th Line;—The candle stick.

Inter.;— Mark time, in place, three counts. (Left; right and left.)

Repeat back to original position.

HUMPTY DUMPTY

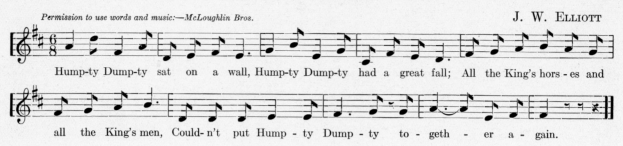

Permission to use words and music:—McLoughlin Bros.

J. W. ELLIOTT

Hump-ty Dump-ty sat on a wall, Hump-ty Dump-ty had a great fall; All the King's hors-es and

all the King's men, Could-n't put Hump-ty Dump-ty to-geth-er a-gain.

DESCRIPTION

MISS A. E. BARTH

Formation;—Standing in the right aisle at attention.

1st Line;—Humpty Dumpty sat on a wall,

Interpretation;—Upon the word, "sat," pupils sit upon own desks; feet hanging in aisle.

2nd Line;—Humpty Dumpty had a great fall;

Inter.;— Upon the word, "fall," pupils jump into the right aisles; bending knees deeply, facing the front of the room.

3rd Line;—All the King's horses and all the King's men,

Inter.;— Assume position of attention with arms stretched forward holding imaginary reins, at the same time "marking time" (ten counts), raising knees waist high.

4th Line;—Couldn't put Humpty Dumpty together again.

Inter.;— Shaking the head in sorrow; right, left, right and front. Hands are placed upon hips during this movement.

HUMPTY DUMPTY SAT ON A WALL

DICKORY, DICKORY, DOCK

First Verse

J. W. ELLIOTT

Dick - o - ory, dick - o - ory, dock; The mouse ran up the clock; The

clock struck, One, The mouse ran down; Dick - o - ry, dick - o - ry, dock.

DESCRIPTION

Formation;—Standing in the right aisle at attention.

1st Line;—Dickory, dickory, dock;

Interpretation;—Hands clasped overhead; swaying right, left and erect.

2nd Line;—The mouse ran up the clock;

Inter.;—   Upon the word, "ran," stand in own seats with the arms stretched sideward.

3rd Line;—The clock struck, One,

Inter.;—   Upon the word, "One," clap hands overhead and lower arms sideward.

The mouse ran down;

Inter.;—   Upon the word, "ran," jump into the left aisle with hands clasped overhead.

4th Line;—Dickory, dickory, dock.

Inter.;—   Swaying right, left and erect.

Repeat activity to the right, bringing all pupils back to former aisles.

THE PENDULUM

DICKORY, DICKORY, DOCK

Second Verse—Music on Page 25

DESCRIPTION

Formation;—Standing in the right aisle at attention.

1st Line;—Dickory, dickory, dock,

Interpretation;—Hands clasped overhead; swaying right, left and erect.

2nd Line;—"Why scamper," said the clock.

Inter.;— Place hands on hips; execute six running steps forward. (Seven counts.) (Left; right; left; right; left; right; close left to right, completing the movement.)

3rd Line;—You   scared   me so,

Inter.;— Execute ½ turn right about.

          I'll   have to go;

Inter.;— Execute three running steps forward. (Four counts.) (Left; right; left, and close right to left, completing the movement.)

4th Line;—Dickory, dickory, dock.

Inter.;— Hands clasped overhead; swaying right, left and erect.

Repeat to bring the class back to the original position.

LITTLE MISS MUFFET

Arr. by J. N. RICHARDS

Lit - tle Miss Muf - fet sat on a tuf - fet, eat - ing of curds and whey, A - long came a spi - der And sat down be - side her; And fright - en'd Miss Muf - fet a - way. Dear me! Dear me! Dear me! Dear me!

DESCRIPTION

Miss A. E. BARTH

Formation;—Standing in the right aisle at attention. Alternate aisles act as Miss Muffet; other aisles act as the Spider. (Count off from left flank by twos. No. 1—Miss Muffet. No. 2—The Spider.)

1st Line;—Little Miss Muffet sat on a tuffet, eating of curds and whey.

Interpretation;—Upon the word, "sat," Little Miss Muffet climbs into her own seat, faces back of room and sits upon the right side of desk. Hold imaginary plate in left arm and imitate eating.

2nd Line;—Along came a spider

Inter.;— Upon the word, "Along," the Spider hastens over own seat and Miss Muffet's aisle; climbs upon seat and sits with Miss Muffet.

3rd Line;—And sat down beside her;

Inter.;— Completion of second line activity.

4th Line;—And frighten'd Miss Muffet away.

Inter.;— Upon the word, "frighten'd," children return to own seats.

Upon returning to their own seats the children sing—Dear me! Dear me! Dear me! Dear me!

ALONG CAME A SPIDER
(Spiders vaulting seats)

JACK AND JILL

Arr. by J. N. RICHARDS

Jack and Jill went up the hill, to fetch a pail of wa - ter; Jack fell down and

broke his crown, And Jill came tumb - ling af - ter, Boo - hoo! Boo - hoo! Boo - hoo! Boo - hoo!

DESCRIPTION

Miss A. E. BARTH

Formation;—Standing in the right aisle at attention. Alternate aisles act as Jack. (Girls and boys.) Other aisles act as Jill. (Girls and boys.) Count off from left flank by twos. No. 1—Jill. No. 2—Jack.

1st Line;—Jack and Jill went up the hill,

Interpretation;—Upon the word, "up," Jack and Jill take hold of hands and climb into same seats. (The climbing of the hill.)

2nd Line;—To fetch a pail of water;

Inter.;— No activity.

3rd Line;—Jack fell down and broke his crown,

Inter.;— Upon the word, "fell," Jack falls (jumps) into own aisle, bends knees, deeply covering his face with his hands, imitating crying.

4th Line;—And Jill came tumbling after.

Inter.;— Upon the word, "tumbling," Jill falls (jumps) into the same aisle as Jack; bends knees, deeply covering her face with her hands, imitating crying.

Upon completion of the song all children return to their own seats, singing— Boo-hoo! Boo-hoo! Boo-hoo! Boo-hoo!

JACK AND JILL WENT UP THE HILL

BYE O BABY BUNTING

Arr. by J. N. RICHARDS

Bye O Ba - by Bunt - ing, Dad - dy's gone a - hunt - ing; To

fetch a lit - tle rab - bit skin To wrap the Ba - by Bunt - ing in.

DESCRIPTION

Formation;—Standing in the right aisle at attention.

1st Line;—Bye O   Baby   Bunt-   ing

Interpretation;—Hold the baby in the arms, looking down at it, and sway gently to the right.   Sway gently to the left.   Sway gently to the right.   Assume stationary position.

2nd Line;—Daddy's gone a-hunting;

Inter.;— Mark time, in place, seven counts; carry gun over the right shoulder (flex right arm; place hand on shoulder with fingers clenched, forefinger extended to represent barrel of gun.)

3rd Line;—To fetch a little rabbit skin

Inter.;— Kneel on left knee and extend the right arm forward, representing the aiming of a gun. (Fingers of the right hand clenched, with forefinger extended; left hand resting on right upper arm.)

4th Line;—To wrap the Baby Bunting in.

Inter.;— Assume erect position; bend forward and encircle body with arms and return hands to hips upon completion of the sentence.

AIMING THE GUN

LITTLE BOY BLUE

Permission to use words and music:—D. Appleton and Co.

Lit - tle Boy Blue, come blow up your horn, There's sheep in the mead - ow and cows in the corn;

Where is the boy that looks af - ter the sheep? He's un - der the hay - cock fast a - sleep.

DESCRIPTION

Formation;—Standing in the right aisle at attention with hands on hips.

1st Line;—Little Boy Blue, come blow up your horn,

Interpretation;—Mark time, in place. (Four counts.) Upon the word, "blow," hands clenched, elbows raised high, imitate the blowing of the horn. Finish with hands on hips.

2nd Line;—There's sheep in the meadow and cows in the corn;

Inter.;— Upon the word, "sheep," point to the right and look in direction pointed. Upon the word, "cows," replace right hand to hip; point to the left and look in direction pointed. Finish with hands on hips and eyes front.

3rd Line;—Where is the boy that looks after the sheep?

Inter.;— Upon the word, "where," shade the eyes with the right hand and look to the right. Upon the word, "looks," replace right hand to hip; shade the eyes with the left hand and look to the left. Finish with left hand on hip and eyes front.

4th Line;—He's under the haycock fast asleep.

Inter.;— Upon the word, "under," resume seats and lower head to desks upon folded arms.

THERE'S SHEEP IN THE MEADOW

WEE WILLIE WINKIE

Arr. by J. N. Richards

Wee Wil - lie Win - kie runs thru the town, Up - stairs and down - stairs

in his night - gown; Rap - ping at the win - dow, Cry - ing thru the lock:—

Are all the chil - dren in their beds? Now 'tis eight o' - clock.

DESCRIPTION

Formation;—Standing in the right aisle with hands on hips.

1st Line;—Wee Willie Winkie runs through the town,
Interpretation;—Mark time, in place. (Knees waist high.) (Seven counts.)

2nd Line;—Upstairs   and   downstairs
Inter.;—   Heels raised.   Bend knees deeply.

        in his night-   gown;
Inter.;—   Stretch knees, lower heels and bow.   Assume erect position.

3rd Line;—Rapping at the window,
Inter.;—   With hands clenched, stretch arms upward and tap imaginary window. (Four times.)

        Crying through the lock:—
Inter.;—   Cup hands and carry to mouth as if calling, bending knees deeply.

4th Line;—"Are all the children   in their beds?
Inter.;—   Turn head to the right.   Turn head to the left.

        Now 'tis eight o'clock."
Inter.;—   Stretch the knees and lower heels.

HEY, DIDDLE, DIDDLE

Arr. by J. N. RICHARDS

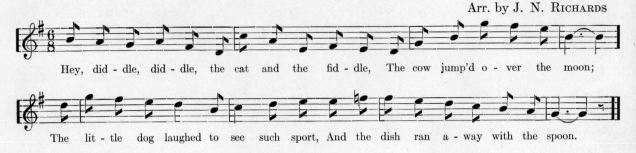

Hey, did - dle, did - dle, the cat and the fid - dle, The cow jump'd o - ver the moon;

The lit - tle dog laughed to see such sport, And the dish ran a - way with the spoon.

DESCRIPTION

Formation;—Standing in the right aisle at attention with hands on hips.

1st Line;—Hey, diddle, diddle,   the cat   and   the fiddle,

Interpretation;—Mark time, in place, five counts.   Imitate the action of playing the fiddle. One upward stroke of the bow.   One downward stroke of the bow.

2nd Line;—The cow   jumped over   the moon;

Inter.;—   Turn to the left; place hands on edge of desk and back of seat and bend knees slightly.   Vault over the seat.   Turn to the right (front); stretch knees, lower heels and place hands on hips.

3rd Line;—The little dog   laughed to see   such sport,

Inter.;—   Bend trunk forward, hugging self, imitating great hilarity.   Assume erect position with hands on hips.

4th Line;—And the   dish ran away with the spoon.

Inter.;—   Execute a complete turn to the right with seven running steps, terminating action upon the word, "spoon."

Stamp feet twice, in place, at the completion of the entire activity.

WHERE HAS MY LITTLE DOG GONE?

Permission to use words and music:—Miss Lydia Clark and Benj. H. Sanborn & Co.

Arr. by Fannie Robertson

Oh where, oh where has my little dog gone? Oh where, oh where has he gone?

With his tail cut short and his ears cut long, Oh where, oh where has he gone?

DESCRIPTION

Formation;—Standing in the right aisle at attention with hands on hips.

1st Line;—Oh where,   oh where   has my little   dog gone?

Interpretation;—Shade eyes with the right hand and with a jump execute ¼ turn to the right.

With a jump execute ¼ turn to the left. (Front.)

With a jump execute ¼ turn to the left.

With a jump execute ¼ turn to the right. (Front.)

2nd Line;—Oh where   oh where   has he   g-   one?

Inter.;—Replace right hand to hip; shade eyes with the left hand and with a jump execute ¼ turn to the left.

With a jump execute ¼ turn to the right (Front.)

With a jump execute ¼ turn to the right.

With a jump execute ¼ turn to the left (Front.)

3rd Line;—With his tail cut short and his ears cut long,

Inter.;—Upon the word, "tail," bend forward, placing hands behind back (palms together; fingers extended.)

Upon the words, "and his," assume erect position with hands at sides.

Upon the word, "ears," raise arms sideward, placing thumbs in ears (fingers extended.)

4th Line;—Oh where,   oh where   has he   gone?

Inter.;—Replace left hand to hip; shade eyes with the right hand and with a jump execute ½ turn right about.

With a jump execute ½ turn right about. (Front.)

Replace right hand to hip, bow and assume erect position.

LOOKING FOR THE DOG

RIDE A COCK-HORSE

Arr. by J. N. Richards

Ride a Cock-horse to Ban-bur-y Cross, To see a fine la-dy up-on a white horse,

Rings on her fin-gers and bells on her toes, She shall have mu-sic wher-ev-er she goes.

DESCRIPTION

Formation;—Standing in the right aisle at attention with hands on hips.

1st Line;—Ride a Cock-horse to Banbury Cross,

Interpretation;—Stretch arms forward, holding imaginary reins; bending and stretching knees. (Three times.)

2nd Line;—To see a fine lady upon a white horse,

Inter.;— Replace left hand to hip; shade the eyes with the right hand and rotate the body to the right upon the word, "To." Replace the right hand to hip; shade the eyes with the left hand and rotate the body to the left upon the word, "upon." Replace the left hand to hip and turn the body forward upon the word, "horse."

3rd Line;—Rings on her fingers and bells on her toes,

Inter.;— Raise arms forward, palms forward, fingers and thumbs extended upon the word, "Rings." Bend the trunk slightly forward and lower arms (palms forward), looking at the toes, upon the word, "bells." Assume erect position with hands on hips, upon the word, "toes."

4th Line;—She shall have music wherever she goes.

Inter.;— Wave the baton with the right hand (forefinger extended; thumb and remaining fingers clenched) to the left, right, left, right and left, upon the words, "She shall have music." (Five counts.)
Replace the right hand to hip, bow and assume erect position upon the words, "wherever she goes."

THE SALUTE (*See page 35*)   THE RIDING OF THE HORSE

YANKEE DOODLE

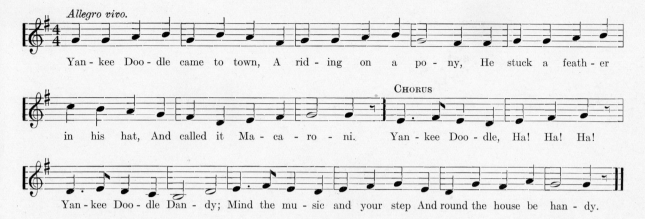

Yan-kee Doo-dle came to town, A rid-ing on a po-ny, He stuck a feath-er in his hat, And called it Ma-ca-ro-ni. Yan-kee Doo-dle, Ha! Ha! Ha! Yan-kee Doo-dle Dan-dy; Mind the mu-sic and your step And round the house be han-dy.

DESCRIPTION

Formation;—Standing in the right aisle at attention with hands on hips.

Verse

1st Line;—Yankee Doodle came to town,

Interpretation;—Children mark time, in place. (Seven counts.)

2nd Line;—A riding on a pony,

Inter.;— Stretching arms forward as if holding imaginary reins; bend and stretch knees (four times), finishing with hands on hips.

3rd Line;—He stuck a feather in his hat,

Inter.;— Upon the word, "stuck," take off the hat with the left hand and upon the word, "in," insert the feather. Finish with hands on hips.

4th Line;—And called it Macaroni.

Inter.;—Mark time, in place. (Eight counts.)

Chorus

1st Line;—Yankee Doodle,

Inter.;— Mark time, in place. (Four counts.)

Ha! Ha! Ha!

Clap hands, three times. Finish with hands on hips.

2nd Line;—Yankee Doodle

Inter.;— Mark time, in place. (Four counts.)

Dandy.

Bow and assume erect position.

3rd Line;—Mind the music

Inter.;— Wave the baton with right hand (forefinger extended) left, right, left and right. (Four counts.) Finish with hands on hips.

and your step

Mark time, in place. (Three counts.)

4th Line;—And round the house be handy.

Inter.;— Upon the word, "round," execute a half turn to the right about by jumping. Upon the word, "house," execute a half turn to the right about by jumping. Upon the word, "handy," jump, in place, three times and salute with the right hand.

PAT - A - CAKE

Arr. by J. N. RICHARDS

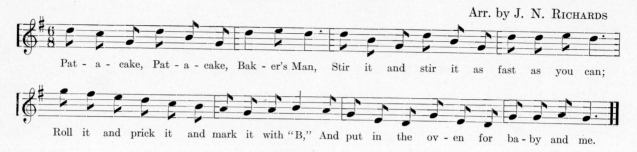

Pat - a - cake, Pat - a - cake, Bak - er's Man, Stir it and stir it as fast as you can;

Roll it and prick it and mark it with "B," And put in the ov - en for ba - by and me.

DESCRIPTION

Formation;—Standing in the right aisle at attention with hands on hips. Count off by twos from left to right and have "ones" face to the right and "twos" face to the left. (Open line formation; partners facing each other.)

1st Line;—Pat-a-cake,   Pat-a-cake,   Baker's Man,

Interpretation;—Clap own hands three times.   Clap partner's hands three times.   Hands hips; bow and assume erect position.

2nd Line;—Stir it and stir it as fast as you can;

Inter.;—Hold imaginary bowl in the left arm (shoulder high), stirring with the right hand, increasing revolutions upon the word, "fast." Upon the word, "can," the hands return to hips.

3rd Line;—Roll it and prick it and mark it with "B";

Inter.;—Upon the words, "roll it," raise hands (palms together; right hand on top) shoulder height, and roll it by a sliding movement.

Upon the words, "prick it," suit action to the words and prick cake, using forefinger of right hand, pressing same into left palm.

Upon the words, "mark it," join forefingers with thumbs, raising to eye height and form letter "B." (Deaf and dumb alphabet.)

4th Line;—And put in the oven for baby and me.

Inter.;—Upon the word, "put," imitate the action of placing the cake in the oven by extending arms forward (palms up) and bending knees. Assume erect position with hands on hips upon the word, "oven."

Upon the word, "baby," bow and assume erect position.

Upon the word, "me," raise the right arm (shoulder height) and place forefinger on chest.

Position.

PAT-A-CAKE

BEAN PORRIDGE

Arr. by J. N. RICHARDS

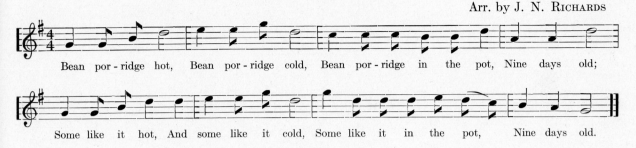

Bean por - ridge hot, Bean por - ridge cold, Bean por - ridge in the pot, Nine days old;

Some like it hot, And some like it cold, Some like it in the pot, Nine days old.

DESCRIPTION

Formation;—Standing in the right aisle in partner formation (open line formation; partners facing), with hands on hips.

Files numbered from the left flank by twos.   No. Ones face to the right; No. Twos face to the left.

1st Line;—Bean   porridge   hot,
Interpretation;—Clap hands to thighs.   Clap own hands.   Clap partner's hands.

Bean   porridge   cold,
Inter.;—   Clap hands to thighs.   Clap own hands.   Clap partner's hands.

2nd Line;—Bean   porridge   in the   pot,
Inter.;—   Clap hands to   Clap own hands.   With right hand clap   Clap own hands.
                 thighs.   partner's right
                                                            hand.

Nine   days   old;
Inter.;—   With left hand clap part-   Clap own hands.   Clap partner's hands.
                 ner's left hand.
                          Description of pupil;—Number Two.
                          Number One;—Counterlike.

3rd Line;—Some   like it   hot, And
Inter.;—   Clasp partner's hands and   Close left to right.   Step dip, right.
                 raise arms to shoulder
                 height.   Step sideward
                 right.

some   like it   cold,
Inter.;—   Step sideward left.   Close right to left.   Step dip, left.

4th Line;—Some   like it   in the   pot,
Inter.;—   Face to the right;   Step forward, left.   Step forward, right.   Close left to right and
                 place right hand   place left hand on
                 on hip, inner   hip.
                 hands joined and
                 raised shoulder
                 height. Step for-
                 ward, right.

Nine days   old.
Inter.;—   With a jump execute a half turn right about.   With a jump execute a half turn right about.

FLY AWAY JACK AND JILL

Arr. by J. N. RICHARDS

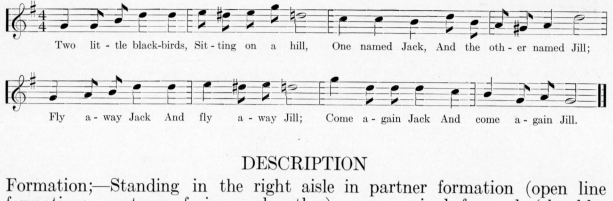

DESCRIPTION

Formation;—Standing in the right aisle in partner formation (open line formation; partners facing each other); arms raised forward (shoulder height) and clasp partner's hands.

NOTE.—If desk width is too great have pupils place hands on hips.

"Count off" from the left flank by twos.

No. 1:—Jack.   No. 2:—Jill.

1st Line;—Two   little   black   -   birds

Interpretation;—Left file (Jack); | Close right to left. | Step sideward, left. | Close right to left.
Step sideward, left.

Inter.;—   Right file (Jill); | Close left to right. | Step sideward, right. | Close left to right.
Step sideward, right.

2nd Line;—Sitting   on   a hill,

Inter.;—   Left file (Jack); | Stamp right. | Replace hands to hips and bend knees deeply.
Stamp left.

Inter.;—   Right file (Jill); | Stamp left. | Replace hands to hips and bend knees deeply.
Stamp right.

3rd Line;—One named   Jack,

Inter.;—   Left file (Jack); Stretch knees   Bow and assume erect position.
and turn to the left.

Inter.;—   Right file (Jill);   No activity.
No activity.

4th Line;—And the   other named   Jill;

Inter.;—   No activity for either files.   Right file (Jill); Stretch   Bow and assume erect position.
knees and turn to the
right.

Inter.;—   Left file (Jack);
No activity.

5th Line;—Fly away, Jack   And   fly away, Jill,

Inter.;—   Left file (Jack); face to the right and   Right file (Jill); face to the left and
execute three chasses to the left.   execute three chasses to the right.

Inter.;—   Right file (Jill);   Left file (Jack);
No activity.   No activity.

6th Line;—Come again, Jack   And   come again, Jill.

Inter.;—   Left file (Jack); Three   Right file (Jill); Three
chasses to the right.   chasses to the left.

Inter.;—   Right file (Jill);   Left file (Jack);
No activity.   No activity.

DIDDLE, DIDDLE DUMPLING

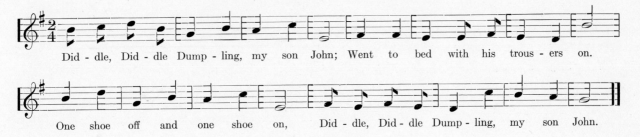

Did - dle, Did - dle Dump - ling, my son John; Went to bed with his trous - ers on.

One shoe off and one shoe on, Did - dle, Did - dle Dump - ling, my son John.

DESCRIPTION

Formation;—Standing in the right aisle in partner formation. Open line formation; partners facing each other; arms raised forward (shoulder height) and clasp partner's hands.

NOTE.—If desk width is too great have pupils place hands on hips.
NOTE.—Description of movement of pupil facing to the left. Movements of partner;—reverse.

1st Line;—Diddle, Diddle Dumpling,

Interpretation;—Step throw, right and left. (Four counts.)

my son John;

Stamp feet; right, left, right and hold. (Four counts.)

2nd Line;—Went to bed with his

Inter.;— Step throw, left and right. (Four counts.)

trousers on.

Replace left foot, bend knees deeply; lower arms with hands clenched. Stretch knees, pulling trousers on and place hands on hips. (Two counts per movement; four counts in all.)

3rd Line;—One shoe off and

Inter.;— Arms raised forward (shoulder height) and clasp partner's hands. Step right sideward and close left to right and step throw, right. (Schottische.). (Four counts.)

one shoe on,

Step left sideward and close right to left and step throw, left. (Schottische.) (Four counts.)

4th Line;—Diddle, Diddle

Inter.;— Jump, in place, once. (Two counts.)

Dumpling

Jump, in place, once. (Two counts.)

my son John.

Jump, in place, three times and hold. (Four counts.)

SING A SONG OF SIXPENCE (*See page 40*)

SING A SONG OF SIXPENCE

Permission to use words and music:—McLoughlin Bros.

J. W. ELLIOTT

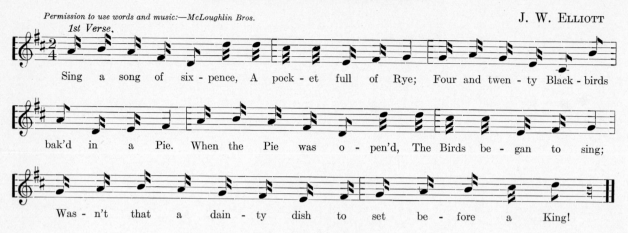

Sing a song of six-pence, A pock-et full of Rye; Four and twen-ty Black-birds

bak'd in a Pie. When the Pie was o-pen'd, The Birds be-gan to sing;

Was-n't that a dain-ty dish to set be-fore a King!

DESCRIPTION

Formation;—Standing in the right aisle facing each other with hands on hips. (Open line formation; partners facing each other.)

1st Line;—Sing a song of sixpence,

Interpretation;—Step to the right, place left toe behind right heel, bending both knees slightly. Repeat to the left. (Cues;—Step and bend and step and bend.)

2nd Line;—A pocket full of Rye;

Inter.;— Execute three slides to the right and bring heels together on the fourth count. (Cues;— Slide, slide, slide and heels.)

3rd Line;—Four and twenty Blackbirds,

Inter.;— Repeat the activity of the first line, starting to the left.

4th Line;—Bak'd in a Pie.

Inter.;— Repeat activity of the second line to the left.

5th Line;—When the Pie was open'd,

Inter.;— Pupils face forward; raise arms forward (shoulder height) in circle form and then extend sideward, imitating the opening of the pie.

6th Line;—The Birds began to sing;

Inter.;— Fluttering of arms up and down, imitating the flying of birds.

7th Line;—Wasn't that a dainty dish

Inter.;— Replace both hands to hips on the word, "dainty." Upon the word, "dish," stretch the right hand forward as if holding the dish and nod the head in approval.

8th Line;—To set before a King!

Inter.;— Step sideward to the right, close feet and bow with arms stretched sideward.

SING A SONG OF SIXPENCE

(*Continued*)

J. W. ELLIOTT

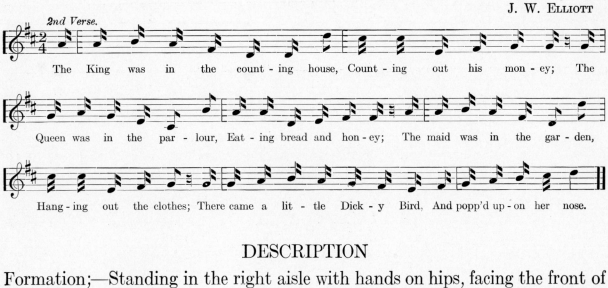

2nd Verse.

The King was in the count - ing house, Count - ing out his mon - ey; The

Queen was in the par - lour, Eat - ing bread and hon - ey; The maid was in the gar - den,

Hang - ing out the clothes; There came a lit - tle Dick - y Bird, And popp'd up - on her nose.

DESCRIPTION

Formation;—Standing in the right aisle with hands on hips, facing the front of room.

1st Line;—The King   was in   the counting   house,

Interpretation;—Jump, in place, with a quarter turn to the right. | Jump, in place, with a quarter turn to the left. (Front.) | Place left foot in seat area. | Sit in seat.

Counting out his money;

Inter.;— Suit activity to words, holding imaginary coins in palm of left hand and count with the right hand.

2nd Line;—The Queen   was in   the parlour,

Inter.;— Stand in the right aisle; face to the left and immediately place hands in support on back of seat and edge of desk. | Vault over seat. (Upon completion of vault, the hands assume normal position.) | Face to the right; place right foot in seat area and become seated.

Eating bread and honey;

Inter.;— Suit activity to words, encircling imaginary plate with left arm and imitate eating with the right hand.

3rd Line;—The maid   was in   the garden,

Inter.;— Place right foot in right aisle. | Stand in right aisle and place hands on hips. | Bow and assume erect position.

Hanging   out   the clothes;

Inter.;— Bend trunk forward downward; stretch arms downward, grasping clothes. | Raise trunk, stretch arms upward and grasp imaginary clothesline. | Using right hand, take clothespin out of mouth and pin clothes on the line.

4th Line;—There came a little Dicky Bird,

Inter.;— Replace hands to hips and mark time, in place. (Left, right, left and right.)

And popped   upon her   nose!

Inter.;— Jump, in place, and clap hands once. | Replace hands to hips; step right sideward and close left to right. | Bow and assume erect position.

SEE SAW, MARJORY DAW

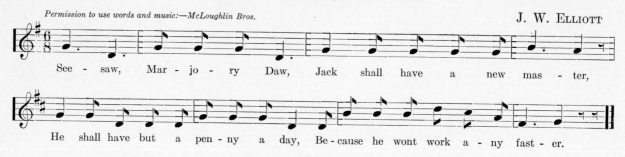

Permission to use words and music:—McLoughlin Bros.

J. W. ELLIOTT

See - saw, Mar - jo - ry Daw, Jack shall have a new mas - ter,

He shall have but a pen - ny a day, Be - cause he wont work a - ny fast - er.

DESCRIPTION

Formation;—Arrange class so that three aisles may work together.

    Center aisle;—Jump to stride stand with arms raised sideward.

    Outer aisles;—Face the center and grasp with both hands the outstretched hand of pupil in center.

    The center player acts as the Board; outer players as riders.

1st Line;—See Saw, Marjory Daw,

Interpretation;—Center activity;—Pupil bends trunk to the right, left, right and left.

    Outer aisles;— When center pupils bend to the right, the children on the right act as riders on board, bending and stretching knees. In reversing the movement, similar activity for those on the left.

2nd Line;—Jack shall have a new master,

Inter.;— Center and outer aisles activity;—Continue movement as described for the first line, finishing in erect position with hands on hips.

3rd Line;—He shall have but a penny a day,

Inter.;— Outer aisles;— Placing left hand to right elbow, shake index finger three times upon the words, "he shall have"; repeat motion with the left hand upon the words, "but a penny a day." Finish with hands on hips.

    Center activity;—Nod to the right upon the words, "he shall have"; assume erect position and nod to the left upon the words, "but a penny a day." Finish with hands on hips.

4th Line;—Because he won't work any faster.

Inter.;— Repeat activity of first line. (Center and outer aisles.)

Circle

(Outer aisles of classroom or in open area.)

Note.—The following Rhythm Plays are suitable to any open area.

LITTLE JACK HORNER

Permission to use words and music:—McLoughlin Bros.

Arr. by J. W. ELLIOTT

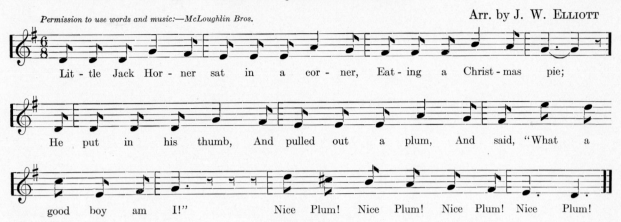

Lit-tle Jack Hor-ner sat in a cor-ner, Eat-ing a Christ-mas pie;

He put in his thumb, And pulled out a plum, And said, "What a

good boy am I!" Nice Plum! Nice Plum! Nice Plum! Nice Plum!

DESCRIPTION

Formation;—Single circle formation facing line of direction with hands on hips.

1st Line;—Little   Jack Horner   sat in a   corner,

Interpretation;—Step forward, right.   Step forward, left.   Step forward, right, turn to the left, closing left foot to right foot.   Bend knees deeply.

2nd Line;—Eating a Christmas pie;

Inter.;—   Upon the word, "eating," children encircle imaginary plate with the left arm and imitate eating with the right hand.

3rd Line;—He put in his thumb, And pulled out a plum,

Inter.;—   Upon the word, "put," children imitate the action of putting thumb in pie and pulling out a plum, making the action vigorous upon the word, "pulled," stretching the arm overhead. Look at plum.

4th Line;—And said, "What a good boy am I!"

Inter.;—   Proudly pats the chest with the left hand.

Conclusion;—Nice Plum!   Nice Plum!   Nice Plum!   Nice Plum!

Inter.;—   Lowers plum to mouth, imitating eating, tapping the chest the while.

THE SPIDER FRIGHTENING MISS MUFFET
(See page 46)

LITTLE MISS MUFFET

Arr. by J. N. RICHARDS

Lit-tle Miss Muf-fet sat on a tuf-fet, eat-ing of curds and whey, A-

long came a spi-der And sat down be-side her; And frighten'd Miss Muf-fet a-way.

DESCRIPTION

Formation;—Double circle formation facing line of direction with hands on hips.

　Inner circle:—The Spider.

　Outer circle:—Miss Muffet.

　Suggestion;—In so far as possible have the boys form the inner circle and the girls the outer circle.

1st Line;—Little Miss Muffet sat on a   **tuffet,**

Interpretation;—Outer circle (Miss Muffet); starting with the right foot execute   Bend knees deeply.
　　　three steps in line of direction. (Right; left; right and close
　　　left to right.)

Inter.;—   Inner circle (Spider); No activity.

eating of curds and whey,

Inter.;—   Hold imaginary plate in the left hand (palm up) and imitate eating. Hands are replaced to
　　　hips upon the completion of the word, "whey."

Inter.;—   Inner circle (Spider); No activity.

2nd Line;—Along came a spider

Inter.;—   Inner circle (Spider); Starting with the left foot execute five running steps in line of
　　　direction. (This should bring partners together.)

Inter.;—   Outer circle (Miss Muffet); No activity.

3rd Line;—And   **sat**   **down beside her;**

Inter.;—   Inner circle (Spider); Bend   Spring upward and upon
　　　knees slightly.   return bend knees deep-
　　　　　　　　　　　ly and face partner.
　　　　　　　　　　　Raise hands, fingers ex-
　　　　　　　　　　　tended and flexed. (Eye
　　　　　　　　　　　height.)

And   **sat down beside her;**

Inter.;—   Outer circle (Miss Muffet); Turns head to
　　　the left, holds hands in position to ward
　　　off attack of the Spider.

4th Line;—And   **frighten'd**   **Miss Muffet away.**

Inter.;—   Outer circle (Miss Muffet); Place hands on hips;
　　　stretch knees and with six running steps encircle
　　　the Spider and return to place.

Inter.;—   Inner circle (Spider); No activity.

JACK AND JILL

Arr. by J. N. Richards

Jack and Jill went up the hill, To fetch a pail of wa-ter; Jack fell down and

broke his crown, And Jill came tum-bling af-ter. Boo-hoo! Boo-hoo! Boo-hoo! Boo-hoo!

DESCRIPTION

Formation;—Double circle formation. Children bend knees deeply; place outside hand on hip and clasp partner's hand.
>Inner circle:—Jill.
>Outer circle:—Jack.

1st Line;—Jack and Jill went up the hill,

Interpretation;—Starting with the left foot marching in line of direction execute three steps, closing right foot to left upon completion of movement. As the steppings are taken, the knees are stretched gradually until reaching erect position.

2nd Line;—To fetch a pail of wa-   ter;

Inter.;—   Bend trunk forward, stretching left arm (hand clenched) downward, holding imaginary pail under spout of pump. Bend right arm (hand clenched) to thrust, grasping the imaginary pump handle. Imitate pumping of water. (Three times.)   Assume erect position with hands on hips.

3rd Line;—Jack fell down and broke his crown,

Activity as applied to children representing Jack. (Outer circle.)

Inter.;— Upon the word, "Jack," bend knees slightly; upon the word, "fell," pupils spring lightly upward and assume deep knee position, placing right hand upon the head (the crown) and left hand upon the floor. (The hand on floor is in the forward plane.)

4th Line;—And Jill came tumbling after.

Activity as applied to children representing Jill. (Inner circle.)

Inter.;— Upon the word, "Jill," bend knees slightly; upon the word, "came," spring lightly upward and assume deep knee position, covering face with right hand (crying) and placing left hand on floor. (The hand on floor is in the forward plane.)

Upon completion of the song all children gradually stretch the knees, shaking the head in sorrow as they sing—Boo-hoo! Boo-hoo! Boo-hoo! Boo-hoo!
>Cover the face with the hands.
>Movement of head;—Right; left; right; left; right; left; right and front.

PUMPING A PAIL OF WATER

DICKORY, DICKORY, DOCK

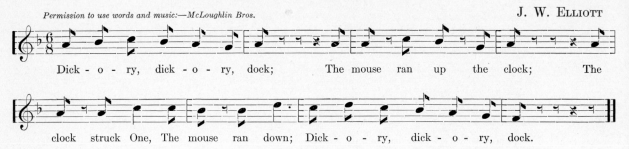

Permission to use words and music:—McLoughlin Bros.

J. W. ELLIOTT

Dick - o - ry, dick - o - ry, dock; The mouse ran up the clock; The

clock struck One, The mouse ran down; Dick - o - ry, dick - o - ry, dock.

DESCRIPTION

Formation;—Single circle facing line of direction with hands on hips.

1st Line;—Dickory,   dickory,   dock;

Interpretation;—Arms stretched overhead with hands clasped. Bend trunk to the left.   Bend trunk to the right.   Assume erect position.

2nd Line;—The   mouse ran up the clock;

Inter.;— Place hands on hips; turn to the left and starting with the left foot execute six running steps forward, closing left foot to right, completing the movement. (Seven counts.)

3rd Line;—The clock   struck   .   One,

Inter.;— Turn right about.   Clap hands overhead and replace to hips.

The   mouse ran   down;

Inter.;— Three running steps forward. (Left; right and left.)   Step forward, right and turn to the left, closing left foot to right foot.

4th Line;—Dickory,   dickory,   dock.

Inter.;— Arms stretched overhead with hands clasped. Bend trunk to the left.   Bend trunk to the right.   Assume erect position.

Position!

LOOBY LOO

Permission to use words and music:—Miss Lydia Clark and Benj. H. Sanborn & Co.

Arr. by FANNIE ROBERTSON

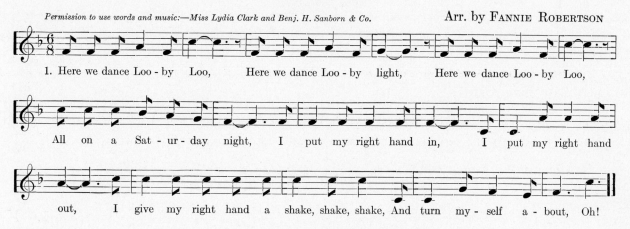

1. Here we dance Loo - by Loo, Here we dance Loo - by light, Here we dance Loo - by Loo,

All on a Sat - ur - day night, I put my right hand in, I put my right hand

out, I give my right hand a shake, shake, shake, And turn my - self a - bout, Oh!

DESCRIPTION

Formation;—Single circle formation, facing counter clock-wise (right), in close order formation. Hands are placed upon the shoulders of the pupil in front.

NOTE.—In classroom:—Single circle around one row of seats.

Verse

Here we dance Looby Loo,
Here we dance Looby Light,
Here we dance Looby Loo,
Every Saturday night.

Interpretation;—Children march in line of direction, starting with inside foot (left), swaying inward (left) and outward (right). Upon the completion of the verse, the children immediately cease the movement and face the center of the circle.

Chorus

I put my right hand in,
I put my right hand out,
I give my right hand a shake, shake, shake,
And turn myself about.   Oh!

Inter.;— Imitate activity as suggested and in turning execute same by spinning about upon the right foot to the right. Upon completion of the turn immediately face line of direction, placing hands upon pupil's shoulders in front in readiness for the verse action.

Chorus

2nd;—I put my left hand in, etc.
3rd;—I put my right foot in, etc.
4th;—I put my left foot in, etc.
5th;—I put my little head in, etc.
6th;—I put my whole self in, etc.

BAA, BAA, BLACK SHEEP

Permission to use words and music:—Miss Lydia Clark and Benj. H. Sanborn & Co.

Arr. by FANNIE ROBERTSON

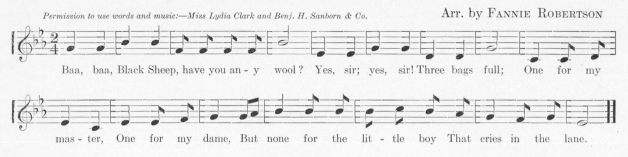

Baa, baa, Black Sheep, have you an - y wool? Yes, sir; yes, sir! Three bags full; One for my

mas - ter, One for my dame, But none for the lit - tle boy That cries in the lane.

DESCRIPTION

Formation;—Children form a single circle with hands joined. (The Sheep.) A boy is chosen who stands in the center of the circle. (The little boy in the lane.) Outer, front and rear aisles of room utilized.

1st Line;—Baa, Baa, Black Sheep, have you any wool?

Interpretation;—Seven quick slides to the right, ceasing movement on the eighth count.

2nd Line;—Yes, sir; yes, sir!

Inter.;— Those in the circle (The Sheep), place hands on hips and nod their heads twice emphatically.

Three bags full;

Inter.;— Place right elbow in left hand with three fingers extended, shaking same three times vigorously.

3rd Line;—One for my master,

Inter.;— Step sideward to the right and close feet; bow and assume erect position. Hands are placed upon the hips.

One for my dame,

Inter.;— Step sideward to the left and close feet; bow and assume erect position. Hands are placed upon hips.

4th Line;—But none for the little boy

Inter.;— Mark time, in place; (right; left; right; left); turning head to the right, left, right and front. Hands are placed on hips.

That cries in the lane.

Inter.;— Place right elbow in the left hand with forefinger extended, shaking same three times vigorously at the little boy in the center of the circle.

THE LITTLE BOY CRYING IN THE LANE

BEAN PORRIDGE

Arr. by J. N. RICHARDS

Bean por - ridge hot, Bean por - ridge cold, Bean por - ridge in the pot, Nine days old;

Some like it hot, And some like it cold, Some like it in the pot, Nine days old.

DESCRIPTION

Formation;—Double circle formation facing partners with hands on hips.

Suggestion:—In so far as possible have the sex units divided; the boys forming the inner circle and the girls forming the outer circle.

1st Line;—Bean   **porridge**   **hot,**

Interpretation;—Clap hands to thighs.   Clap own hands.   Clap partner's hands.

       Bean   **porridge**   **cold,**

Inter.;—   Clap hands to thighs.   Clap own hands.   Clap partner's hands.

2nd Line;—Bean   **porridge**   **in the**   **pot,**

Inter.;—   Clap hands to thighs.   Clap own hands.   With right hand, clap partner's right hand.   Clap own hands.

       Nine   **days**   **old;**

Inter.;—   With left hand clap partner's left hand.   Clap own hands.   Clap partner's hands.

Description of pupil; Outer circle. Counterlike as to movement for pupils of inner circle.

3rd Line;—Some   **like it**   **hot, And**

Inter.;—   Clasp partner's hands and raise arms to shoulder height. Step sideward, right. (In line of direction.)   Close left to right.   Step dip, right.

       Some   **like it**   **cold,**

Inter.;—   Step sideward, left. (In reverse line of direction.)   Close right to left.   Step dip, left.

4th Line;—Some like it in the pot,

Inter.;—   Four chasse steps in line of direction.

       Nine days   **old.**

Inter.;—   Jump, in place, once.   Jump, in place, once.

Lenoir Rhyne College
LIBRARY

FLY AWAY JACK AND JILL

Arr. by J. N. Richards

Two lit - tle black- birds, Sit - ting on a hill, One named Jack And the oth - er named Jill;

Fly a - way, Jack and fly a - way, Jill; Come a - gain, Jack And come a - gain, Jill.

DESCRIPTION

Formation;—Double circle facing counter clockwise (line of direction); inside hands joined and raised shoulder height; outside hands on hips.

Inner circle:—Jack.   Outer circle:—Jill.

Suggestion;—In so far as possible have the sex units divided, the boys forming the inside circle and the girls forming the outside circle.

Start the dance movement with the outside foot. (Boys beginning with the left foot; girls beginning with the right foot.)

1st Line;—Two little blackbirds,

Interpretation;—Three steps in line of direction.
Inner circle (Jack);—(Left; right, left and close right to left.)
Outer circle (Jill);—(Right; left, right and close left to right.)

Sitting on a hill,

Inter.;—   Bend knees deeply. Outer and inner circles.

2nd Line;—One named   Jack

Inter.;—   Inner circle (Jack); place hands on hips,   Bow and assume erect position.
stretch knees and turn to partner.
(Right.)

	One	named Jack
Inter.;— Outer circle (Jill);	Replace left hand to hip and remain in deep knee position.	No activity.

And the   other named   Jill;

Inter.;—   No activity for either cir-   Outer circle (Jill); stretch   Bow and assume erect position.
cles.   knees and turn to part-
ner (Left.)

Inter.;—   Inner circle;—No activity.

3rd Line;—Fly away, Jack   And   fly away, Jill;

Inter.;—   Inner circle (Jack); Three   Outer circle (Jill); Three chasses in line
chasses in line of direc-   of direction.
tion.

Inter.;—   Outer circle (Jill); No ac-   Inner circle (Jack); No activity.
tivity.

Come again, Jack   And   come again, Jill.

Inter.;—   Inner circle (Jack); Three   Outer circle (Jill); Three chasses in
chasses in reverse line of   reverse line of direction.
direction.

Inter.;—   Outer circle (Jill); No ac-   Inner circle (Jack); No activity.
tivity.

TWO LITTLE BLACK BIRDS SITTING ON A HILL
(See page 52)

I HAD A LITTLE PONY
(See page 56)

POP GOES THE WEASEL

A six-pence for a spool of thread, A pen-ny for a need-le; That's the way the mon-ey goes; Pop goes the weas-el. Watch how the need-le does fly, Nim-ble hands to guide it; Eve-ry time the wheel goes round, Pop goes the weas-el.

DESCRIPTION

Formation;—Double circle formation, partners facing; hands joined and raised shoulder height.

Suggestion;—In so far as possible have the sex units divided, the boys forming the inner circle and the girls forming the outer circle.

Description of the pupils occupying the outer circle (girls); inner circle (boys); counterlike.

Verse

1st Line;—A sixpence for   a spool of thread,

Interpretation;—Step dip, right. (In line of direction.)   Step dip, left. (In reverse line of direction.)

2nd Line;—A penny for a needle;

Inter.;—   Four chasse steps in line of direction.

NOTE.—On the fourth chasse step do not close left foot to the right.

3rd Line;—That's   the way   the money   goes;

Inter.;—   Face line of direc-   Step forward, right.   Step forward, left.   Close right to left and tion; inner hands   place inner hand to joined and outer   hip. hands on hips. Step forward, left.

4th Line;—Pop   goes the   weasel.

Inter.;—   With a jump, exe-   With a jump, execute a turn right about, cute a turn right   and clap hands once. Finish with about and clap   inner hands joined and outer hands on hands once.   hips. Facing in line of direction.

POP GOES THE WEASEL
(*Continued*)

Repeat Verse

1st Line;—A sixpence for   **a spool of thread,**
Interpretation;—Two step, right. (In line of direction.)   Two step, left. (In line of direction.)

2nd Line;—A penny   **for a**   **needle;**
Inter.;—   Step forward, right.   Step forward, left.   Step forward, right and close left to right.

3rd Line;—That's the way   **the money goes;**
Inter.;—   Two step, left. (In line of direction.)   Two step, right. (In line of direction.)

4th Line;—Pop   **goes the**   **weasel.**
Inter.;—   Step forward, left.   Step forward, right.   Step forward, left and close right to the left. Finish with hands on hips.

Chorus

1st Line;—Watch how   **the needle does fly,**
Inter.;—   Turn to partner and step dip, right. (In line of direction.) Clap hands three times.   Step dip, left. (In reverse line of direction.) Clap hands three times.

2nd Line;—Nimble hands to guide it;
Inter.;—   Encircle to the right with three walking steps. (Right; left; right and close left to right.) As the first step is taken clap hands once and replace hands to hips.

3rd Line;—Every time   **the wheel goes round,**
Inter.;—   Step dip, left. (In reverse line of direction.) Clap hands three times.   Step dip, right. (In line of direction.) Clap hands three times.

4th Line;—Pop goes the weasel.
Inter.;—   Encircle to the left with three walking steps. (Left; right; left and close right to the left.) As the first step is taken clap hands once and replace hands to hips.

DAPPLE GREY

Arr. by J. N. RICHARDS

I had a lit-tle po-ny And his name was Dap-ple Grey; I lent him to a

la-dy, To ride a mile a-way. She whipped him and she slashed him, She

rode him through the mire; I would not lend my po-ny now For all the la-dy's hire.

DESCRIPTION

Formation;—Children arranged in double circle formation, facing counter clockwise (line of direction); outside hands placed on hips; inside hands joined and raised shoulder height.

Suggestion;—In so far as possible have the sex units divided, the boys forming the inside circle and the girls forming the outside circle.

Start the dance movement with the outside foot. (Boys beginning with the left foot; girls beginning with the right foot.)

Description of pupils in outer circles. (Girls.) Counterlike—Inner

1st Line;—I had   **a little**   **pony**

Interpretation;—Point step forward, right.   Point step backward, right.   Three steps forward and hold. (Right; left and right.)

Cues;—Point and point and step, step, step.

And his name   **was Dapple**   **Grey;**

Inter.;— Swing left forward and point step forward, left.   Point step backward, left.   Three steps forward and hold. (Left; right and left.)

Cues;—Point and point and step, step, step.

2nd Line;—I lent   **him to**   **a lady,**

Inter.;— With a jump, face partner; clasp outside hands and raise both arms to shoulder height.   Jump, in place, once.   Step throw, right and step throw, left.

To ride a mile away.

Inter.;—Seven chasses in line of direction, closing left to right, completing movement.

3rd Line;—She   **whipped him and she slashed him,**

Inter.;— Replace left hand to hip. Grasp imaginary whip with the right hand and with a vigorous motion imitate whipping. (Three times replacing hand to hip upon the word, "him.") Mark time, in place, six counts. (Right; left; right; left; right and left.)

NOTE.—The downward movement of whipping takes place as the right foot is lowered to the floor.

She   **rode him through the mire;**

Inter.;— Clasp partner's hands, raising arms to shoulder height and bend and stretch knees six times.

4th Line;—I would   **not lend**   **my pony now**

Inter.;— Step dip, right, clapping hands three times.   Step dip, left, clapping hands three times.   Face line of direction; replace hands to hips and execute two steps forward. (Right; left and close right to left.)

For all   **the lady's**   **hire.**

Inter.;— Step throw, right.   Step throw, left   Mark time, in place, three counts. (Right; left and right.)

SING A SONG OF SIXPENCE

Permission to use words and music:—McLoughlin Bros.

Arr. by J. W. ELLIOTT

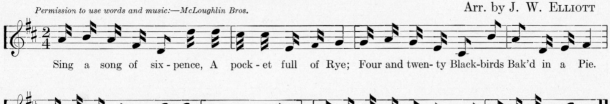

Sing a song of six-pence, A pock-et full of Rye; Four and twen-ty Black-birds Bak'd in a Pie.

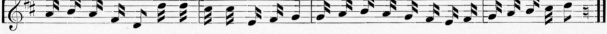

When the Pie was o-pen'd, The Birds be-gan to sing; Was-n't that a dain-ty dish To set be-fore a King.

DESCRIPTION

Formation;—Single circle formation facing counter clockwise (right) in close order formation. Hands are placed upon the shoulders of the pupil in front.

1st Verse

1st Line;—Sing a song of sixpence, A pocket full of Rye;

Interpretation;—Starting with the inside foot (left) moving in line of direction execute point step forward and step, left; right; left and right. During this movement, bend the trunk slightly to the left and right as the activity proceeds.

Cues;—Point and step; point and step; point and step; point and step.

2nd Line;—Four and twenty Blackbirds

Inter.;— Turn the head to the left; step sideward, left and close right to left and repeat.

Cue;—Step and close; step and close.

Bak'd in a Pie.

Inter.;— Turn the head to the right; step sideward, right and close left to the right and repeat.

Cue;—Step and close; step and close.

3rd Line;—When the Pie was open'd,

Inter.;— Facing inward (left); clasp hands to the right and left and starting with the right foot execute three steps backward. (Right; left; right and close left to the right.)

Cues;—Step; step; step and close.

The Birds began to sing;

Inter.;— Three chasse steps in line of direction. (To the right.)

4th Line;—Wasn't that a dainty dish

Inter.;— Extend arms forward slightly flexed, clapping hands seven times, and step bend, left and right. (Step to the left; place the right toe behind the left heel, bending both knees slightly. During this movement the head is turned to the left, the trunk bending slightly as the knee bending occurs. (Counterlike as to movement of head and trunk when executed to the right.)

To set before   **a King?**

Inter.;— Replace hands to hips; step sideward, left and close right to left.

Bow and assume erect position.

SING A SONG OF SIXPENCE (Continued)
Second Verse

J. W. ELLIOTT

The King was in the count - ing house, Count - ing out his mon - ey; The

Queen was in the par - lour, Eat - ing bread and hon - ey; The maid was in the gar - den,

Hang - ing out the clothes; There came a lit - tle Dick - y Bird, And popp'd up - on her nose.

DESCRIPTION

Formation;—Single circle facing inward with hands on hips.

1st Line;—The King was in the counting house,
Interpretation;—Starting with the left foot execute three steps forward. (Left; right; left and close right to the left.)

Counting out his money;
Inter.;— Bend knees deeply and suit activity to the words, holding imaginary coins in the palm of the left hand, counting with the right hand. (Six counts.)

2nd Line;—The Queen was in the parlour,
Inter.;— Stretch the knees, lower heels; facing to the right, start with the right foot, execute three chasse steps to the right, with arms raised sideward.

Eating bread and honey;
Inter.;— Hold imaginary plate in the left hand (palm up) and suit activity to words, imitating eating with the right hand. (Six counts.)

3rd Line;—The maid was in   the garden,
Inter.;— Extend arms forward slightly flexed, clapping hands seven times, and step bend, left and right. (Step to the left, place right toe behind the left heel, bending both knees slightly. During this movement the head is turned to the left, the trunk bending slightly as the knee bending occurs. (Counterlike as to movement of head and trunk when executed to the right.)

Hanging   out   the clothes;
Inter.;— Replace left foot; stretch the knees; bending trunk forward, downward grasping clothes with hands.　Stretching the trunk; raise arms forward upward to imaginary clothesline.　Take clothespin out of mouth with right hand and pin clothes to line.

4th Line;—There came a little Dicky Bird,
Inter.;— Replace hands to hips, execute four hops forward.

And popp'd   upon her nose.
Inter.;— Clap hands, replacing same to hips, and execute one-quarter turn to the left by hopping.　Bow and assume erect position.

Folk Dance Books and Others

Each book contains the music and full descriptions of the dances

BELL
    Fifty Figure and Character Dances. 2 Vols.
        Beautifully Illustrated.....................................Octavo, cloth, per set $8.00

BERGQUIST
    Swedish Folk Dances........................Illustrated. Octavo, cloth 2.00

BREMNER
    Song Games and Ball Games........................Illustrated. Octavo, cloth 2.00
    More Song Games........................Illustrated. Octavo, cloth 2.00

BURCHENAL
    National Dances of Ireland..............Diagrams and Illustrations. Octavo, cloth 3.00

CAMPBELL AND FRAIN
    Fundamental Bar Work and Ballet Technique.................... Octavo, cloth 5.00

COLBY
    Natural Rhythms and Dances........................Illustrated. Octavo, cloth 4.00

CRAMPTON
    The Folk Dance Book........................Octavo, cloth 2.40
    The Second Folk Dance Book........................Illustrated. Octavo, cloth 2.40

CRAMPTON AND WOLLASTON
    The Song Play Book........................Illustrated. Octavo, cloth 2.40

CRAWFORD
    Folk Dances and Games........................Illustrated. Octavo, cloth 2.40
    Dramatic Games and Dances........................Illustrated. Octavo, cloth 2.40
    Rhythms of Childhood........................Illustrated. Octavo, cloth 2.40

FROST
    The Clog Dance Book........................Illustrated. Octavo, cloth 2.40
    Clog and Character Dances........................Illustrated. Octavo, cloth 2.60

GEARY
    Folk Dances of Czecho Slovakia........................Illustrated. Octavo, cloth 2.40

HINMAN
    Gymnastic and Folk Dancing Books. 5 Vols., paper covers.
        Volumes I to IV ....Illustrated. Octavo. Each 1.60
        Volume V........................ 2.00

LINCOLN
    The Festival Book........................Illustrated. Octavo, cloth 2.40

MARSH
    The Dance in Education. Diagrams. Illustrations. Bibliography. Octavo, boxed, cloth 10.00

POHL
    Manual of Dancing Steps........................Diagrams. Octavo, cloth 3.00

RATH
    Aesthetic Dancing, Revised........................Illustrated. Octavo, cloth 2.00

RICHARDS
    Dramatized Rhythm Plays........................Illustrated. Octavo, cloth 2.40

SHAFTER
    Dramatic Dances for Small Children........................Octavo, cloth 2.40

SPERLING
    The Playground Book........................Illustrated. Octavo, cloth 2.40

WOOD
    New Song Plays to Old Tunes...........Illustrations and Diagrams. Octavo, cloth 2.00

Illustrated Catalogue with Table of Contents of each book sent on request

---

A. S. BARNES AND COMPANY, *Publishers*   NEW YORK